D1314547

TAKING CARE OF YOUR

DOG

Joyce Pope

Series consultant: Michael Findlay

Photographs by: Sally Anne Thompson and R T Willbie/Animal Photography

Franklin Watts
London   New York   Toronto   Sydney

230uu

The author
Joyce Pope is Enquiries Officer of the Zoology
Department at the British Museum of Natural History
and also gives regular public lectures to children and
adults on a wide range of subjects.

She is involved with conservation groups and has
written many books on a variety of topics including
European animals, pets and town animals. She is an
enthusiastic pet owner herself and currently keeps
small mammals, two dogs, a cat and a horse.

The consultant
Michael Findlay is a qualified veterinary surgeon whose
involvement has been mainly with pet animals. He is
now an advisor to a pharmaceutical company. He is
involved with Crufts Dog Show each year and is a
member of the Kennel Club. He is president of several
Cat Clubs and is Chairman of the Feline Advisory
Bureau. He currently has three Siamese cats and two
labrador dogs.

© 1986 Franklin Watts

First published in Great
Britain in 1986 by
Franklin Watts
12a Golden Square
London W1

First published in the
United States of America
by
Franklin Watts Inc.
387 Park Avenue South
New York
N.Y. 10016
UK edition:
ISBN 0 86313 363 0
US edition:
ISBN 0–531–10160–6
Library of Congress
Catalog Card Number:
85–51604

Designed by
Ben White

Illustrated by
Hayward Art Group

Additional photographs
Joyce Pope 23, 27b
RSPCA 12

Printed in Belgium

Acknowledgments
The photographers and publishers would like to thank
Mr. Neil Forbes of the Lansdown Veterinary Surgeons,
Stroud, and the families and their pets who participated
in the photographs for this book.

TAKING CARE OF YOUR

DOG

Contents

Introducing pets

Pets can add interest or amusement to our lives. It has been proved that a pet is often helpful to somebody who is alone or unwell. By caring for our pets we can find out about other creatures that share our world.

▽ Dogs make very good pets. They like companionship and most dogs like children and enjoy the same sort of active games, so they fit in well with family life.

The most important thing

When you have a pet you must remember that it is a living creature, not a toy that you can put away when you no longer wish to play with it. If you treat your pet properly it will learn to trust you.

▽ There are more kinds of dogs than any other sort of domestic animal. Most of them can be trained to fit in with humans. Training a dog well can be fun.

Many people think that dogs are the best of all pets. Like human beings they are social animals and can be really good companions.

A dog must have real commitment from you, as it must be fed, groomed and exercised every few days. It can only be happy when it has this attention and company. A dog can live a long time. It may survive for fifteen years, so you must consider that you could have the responsibility for your pet over a

▷ More than any other animal, a dog is a pet for the whole family, as it is likely that they will all play with it, or help with it. Dogs need affection and discipline. This puppy is being cuddled, but it must learn that it must not jump up on to the furniture.

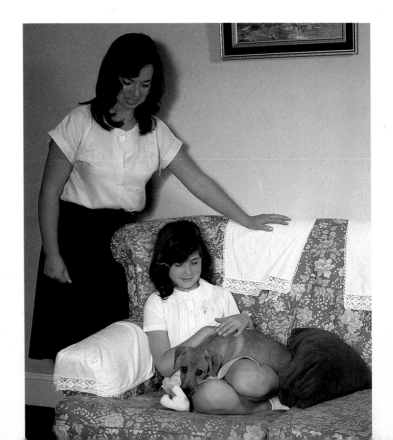

long period of time.

A dog is expensive to feed and keep, so you are bound to need the help of adults in this. A dog can take up a lot of room in a house and it should be able to go outside as well as being taken for walks.

It is not fair on a large dog, to try and keep one in an apartment or a place with no open space around. A dog has to be licensed and you become responsible for it legally, in case it damages property or causes an accident.

▽ Dogs are naturally energetic and most need quite a lot of exercise. They can get this when you walk them and also from play, especially in "fetching" games with sticks or toys. This can be part of the training that they must have if they are to fit into the life of the family.

Dogs as animals

Like wolves, dogs are meat eating hunters which mostly live in a pack. Over time the human family took the place of the pack for the pet dog.

Many breeds of dogs have been developed, ranging in size from giants, which may weigh more than a person, to miniatures or "toy" dogs which may weigh about a pound.

Find out as much as you can about different dog breeds and then decide which you would like to keep.

▽ The beautiful Afghan Hound has a coat which grows continually. It may grow long enough to sweep the ground. It needs an immense amount of grooming to keep it in good condition.

△ The Chihuahua is one of the world's smallest dogs. This may make it a good dog for a family in an apartment.

The very small (toy) breeds would probably be too delicate for the games that you would like to play. It would also be unwise to get one of the very large or strong breeds which you might not be able to control when you were out with it.

Breeds with long hair need a great deal of time spent on grooming them. The best family pets are likely to be short- or rough-coated, medium sized dogs.

▷ You can't be sure what a mixed breed puppy will be like when it grows up, but a mongrel often makes a good pet.

△ The Great Pyrenees weighs over 100 lb (45 kg).

Once everyone has agreed that you may have a dog there are a lot of things that you must do to prepare for it. The most important is to get it a bed. This must be a place that the dog will like to go to, not only to sleep, but a place that you can send it to if you have visitors, or if you need to be quiet when you want to do your work.

For a puppy, a cardboard box well lined with a warm blanket is ideal. Later, when it has finished teething and stopped chewing everything, you can get another sort of bed. But it must be warm and put in a draft-

△ You should try to get a dog bed which will allow the dog to stretch out when it sleeps.

▽ A cardboard box in a warm spot makes a good bed to begin with.

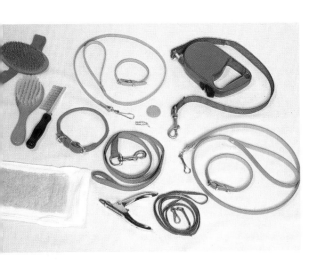

△ Here is a selection of grooming tools and dog collars with identity discs and leashes. Do not get a chain leash which can hurt your dog or damage your hands if you need to shorten it.

△ If you have a small dog your parents may allow you to have a door with a flap, so that it can go outside when it wants to. But before you install this, you must be sure that the area is properly fenced in so that the dog cannot get out into the street.

free spot. The dog's bedding will need to be washed every week, so get something which will wash and dry easily.

You will need a collar with a name tag with your name and address engraved on it. Don't put your dog's name on it. You will also need a leash, preferably a nylon or leather one.

The dog should have special bowls for feeding and drinking from. You should get all of these things before you have the dog. You can get brushes and combs for grooming, and toys a little later on.

Getting a dog

If you go to a dog show or look in as many dog books as possible, you can then decide which dog you want to own. You may have a shock when you try to get one, for pedigree puppies may well cost more than a hundred dollars.

Sadly, many people get dogs and then decide that they don't want them. These dogs often end up as strays. If you cannot afford an expensive dog, you may be able to get one from a shelter.

△ Choosing a dog from a shelter is difficult as they all want you to take them with you. The people who work at the shelter will probably be able to help you so that you don't have the disappointment of having to return a dog which is totally unsuitable for life in your family.

Unwanted and unclaimed dogs are always available from these animal charities and rescue organizations for a small charge or sometimes at no cost at all.

But you must be aware that many adult dogs from such sources may have some unpleasant habits from which they will not easily be cured. It is very important that all dogs from such places should only be taken on the strict condition of one week's trial at home.

▽ Puppies from the same litter may all look very much alike, but they are as different from each other as brothers and sisters are. The breeder should tell you which are the male dogs and which are the females and show you each one separately, so that you can make your choice.

If you go to a dog breeder you should be able to see the mother with her puppies. Go for the lively puppy and not the shy pup cowering at the back of the group. The puppies should be ready to leave their mother when they are over eight weeks old.

You should decide whether you want a male or a female. Females are often quieter and easier to train, but they go into heat twice each year. At this time they are able to mate, so they are very attractive to all the male dogs in the neighborhood. This may cause a nuisance as dogs will be waiting around your house. The breeder will tell you which are the male dogs and which are the females in a litter.

Puppies suffer from illnesses, against which they have to be inoculated. Some illnesses can be passed to human beings, and they may also kill the puppy. If the puppy is old enough, it may have had its first shots before you get it. In this case, you should get its pedigree and transfer papers, and the inoculation certificates.

◁ This is a litter of Corgi puppies. When you buy your puppy you should get papers that show its parentage and what inoculations it has had.

Your new dog

You should take your puppy home in
a carrying case, or carry it to a car.
Until its inoculations are complete
at the age of about 12 weeks, a puppy
may pick up dangerous diseases just
from being where other dogs have
walked.

Remember that your puppy is a
baby that has been taken from its
mother and brothers and sisters.
It will probably be bewildered and a
bit frightened, so you must reassure
it. You will have years in which to
play with your dog so don't try to
play with it right away.

▽ House training is one
of the first lessons for a
dog. It is usually not
difficult as dogs and
puppies want to be clean.
Put a wad of newspaper
by its bed in the
bathroom and more near
to the door for it to use at
night.

It is a good idea to know what you want to call your dog before you get it. Then it won't get confused by lots of different names. Your puppy will learn its name very quickly especially if it is a short one.

Remember to use its name every time you speak to your pet. Your puppy should settle down quite quickly and you can then play gentle games with it.

▽ As soon as your puppy has had a meal, take it out of doors and praise it as soon as it relieves itself. If it has an accident, don't get too upset, but let it know it did wrong. You will have to repeat the praise and scolding until it is house trained.

Your puppy or dog will have to learn many things when it first comes to live with you. But it should not be a one-way process. You, your family and friends must learn to understand your pet as well.

Remember that although it is smart, your dog cannot think like a human being. Always keep anything that you are trying to teach it very simple.

Apart from its name, it must learn some simple words like *no, good dog, come, bed, sit* and *heel*. Teach it to come when you call every time you feed it. You will have to keep repeating the words until your dog

△ A puppy will miss its mother most on the first night that you have it, and it may cry for her. Do not go to it or take it into your bedroom. Give it a hot-water bottle, well wrapped up in a towel to help keep it warm. It will eventually settle down.

▷ Puppies should only go beyond the yard when their inoculations are complete.

learns what to do.

Always praise your dog when it has done anything right. Never hit it, even if it has been naughty – just shake the scruff of the neck gently. It will understand this, for this is what its mother would probably have done to correct it.

Although your puppy may be full of life it needs a great deal of sleep like a human baby, so do not expect it to be active all the time. It should not be taken out for long walks until it is strong enough, probably not before it is several months old.

△ Tiny puppies may have quite sharp teeth so don't let them chew valuable things or things which will harm them.

Feeding your dog

Dogs are meat-eating animals, but if you were to feed your dog on nothing but meat it would become ill, for dogs need a balanced diet. Dogs should have some meat, but they must also have roughage, and carbohydrates and fat which will give them energy.

Vitamins and minerals are added to many dog foods before you buy them. You should not feed your dog

▽ There is a very wide choice of foods for your dog. Meat may be canned or cooked. Carbohydrates may be given as biscuits or meal, which may have added vitamins and minerals. Complete foods are also available.

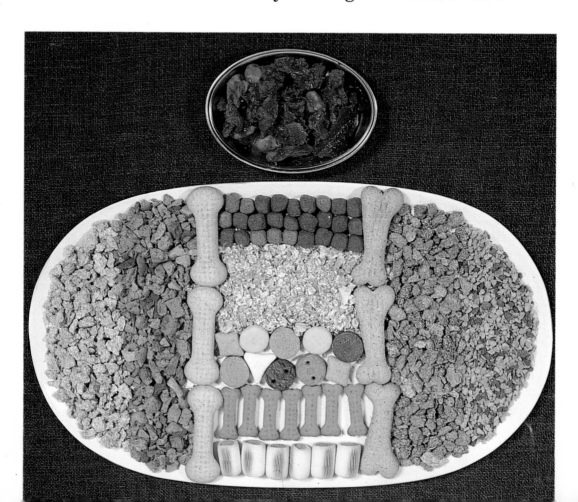

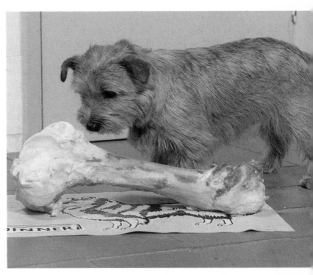

▽ Bones give your dog something interesting to chew and add calcium to its diet. Never give your dog small bones like chicken or rabbit bones, as these splinter.

△ Your dog should have his own food bowl and be fed at the same time and place each day. A puppy needs several meals a day, but as it grows up a dog needs to eat less often. An adult dog should have one meal a day. The dog should always have a bowl of clean water.

only on household scraps. Some of these may certainly be added to your dog's food, but they should not make up more than a small amount of the total. The scraps should be kept until its meal time, never given as snacks, for it is bad for the dog to nibble between meals.

The amount of meat that you give your dog should be about $\frac{1}{3}$oz (20 g) for every pound of its body weight. This should then be about doubled with roughage such as biscuits or dog meal. Your dog may not need as much food as this. If it is getting fat, cut down on the biscuits and increase the exercise.

Dog health

Dogs are usually fairly healthy animals provided that they are fed properly, exercised sensibly and well cared for. However, there are five serious diseases, three of them caused by viruses, which will probably weaken your dog for life, even if it should recover.

Fortunately, diseases can often be prevented by vaccination. But if your dog does not want to eat, or looks unhappy, has a dull coat or runny eyes, you should take it to the

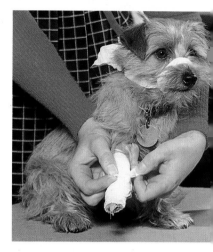

△ You should let the vet examine your dog to check its health as soon as you get it. A dog that is frightened or hurt may bite, so it is wise to make a bandage muzzle, so that it can be treated safely.

◁ Your dog should be inoculated against distemper, hepatitis, and leptospirosis and parvo virus. After its first shots it will need yearly boosters.

veterinarian. The trouble may be dealt with simply, but you could cause needless pain if you delay.

Puppies usually have worms, but these should be dealt with as a routine matter which the breeder or your vet can explain to you and your family. Dogs sometimes get fleas (usually cat fleas) lice or mites, which cause great irritation.

Always check your dog's coat while you are grooming it, so that you are aware of any problems as soon as they happen. Don't let a condition become serious as it is easy to get medication which will deal with these parasites.

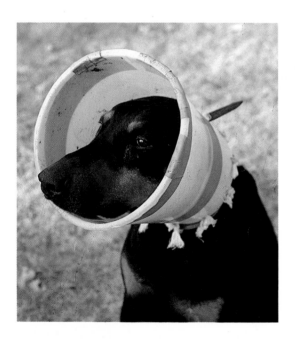

△ This dog has had a minor operation. He is wearing an "Elizabethan collar" made from a bucket, to prevent him from chewing at the stitches on his leg.

Dog hygiene

Dogs keep themselves clean by licking and scratching their fur. Some dogs molt a little all the time. You can help to keep your pet comfortable and your home cleaner by grooming your pet daily to remove loose hair.

A short-haired dog can be groomed quickly with a hound glove. If you have a long-coated dog you will need to have special brushes and combs. Your dog

▽ Be gentle but firm when you groom your dog – it should be something that it looks forward to, not dreads. During the grooming session you should also check that your dog's toenails are not overgrown, and that its ears and teeth are clean.

△ A hound glove is just right for grooming a short haired dog.

△ If your dog smells or has been rolling in something unpleasant you may need to bathe (or wash) it. Always use mild baby shampoo.

△ Large dogs may need to be bathed out of doors in warm weather. Always make sure that they are properly dried off.

may need a bath from time to time.

An important part of hygiene is disposing of your pet's droppings. If possible, you should let it go in your yard, where the droppings can be buried. Never let it foul a sidewalk or park where people walk.

You should train your dog to use the gutter if necessary, when it is outside. If it has an "accident" you should be prepared to clean up the mess with some sort of scoop.

Dogs enjoy tasting and licking things but don't let your dog lick your face. You should always wash your hands after you have been handling or playing with your pet.

Exercise and play

△ A dog can run quite long distances playing in a yard. Many dogs love squeaky toys, but you should watch that your dog has not chewed the toy open, as it might swallow the squeaker, which could harm it.

Most dogs should have exercise. Whatever the weather, they must, provided that they are neither very young puppies nor very old animals, be able to run out of doors. You can let the dog into the yard if you have one, but it should also be taken for longer walks.

Never let a dog out on its own. It might cause an accident, or have a fight, or chase other animals and you would be responsible for it.

Even where there is not a lot of space outside, you can give your dog plenty of exercise by playing with it. Most dogs love fetching sticks and toys, so you can throw things for it to retrieve. Do not use tennis balls, or other small balls, as some dogs can swallow things of this size and choke. It is better to throw a stick or a frisbee. Do not throw stones, as a dog may break its teeth on them.

You will probably want to give your dog some toys. Most dogs chew their toys, so they must be made from quite tough material. Never give your dog a toy which might break into sharp pieces. It might cut itself or be badly injured by swallowing the pieces.

△ In some parks your dog can run as much as it wants to. It will be able to follow the trails of strange dogs or rabbits.

▽ A grown dog will probably enjoy playing with a frisbee, a very hardwearing toy.

Dog obedience

You should train your dog to obey simple commands from the first day that you have it. When you start to take it out, you must teach it to walk on a leash quietly and without pulling.

When you stop to check that the road is clear, the dog should sit by you at the curb until you are able to cross. The dog must also learn to leave other dogs and animals (such as cats or farm stock) alone.

▽ Always keep your dog on a leash in the street. When crossing a road, always halt at the curb and make sure the dog sits until told to cross with you.

You might find it difficult to teach your dog all of these things on your own. In most areas there are dog obedience classes where you can meet people who know a lot about dogs. They will be able to show you how you can help your dog to do the things that you want. Dog training usually involves training the owner as well!

Most dogs want to please their owners and they usually enjoy their training. A well trained, obedient pet is a better companion and is almost certainly happier than an untrained dog.

△ This dog has been trained to walk closely to heel, paying attention to its owner all the time, Once your dog is as good as this, you could enter one of the many competitions held for young handlers. You might become good enough to help other people and dogs in your turn.

Checklist

 Before you get your dog

1 Be sure that you have your parents' permission.
2 Be sure that you have space, especially a place to put the dog's bed.
3 Be sure that you have time to devote to the dog.
4 Be sure that you can afford to keep the dog.
5 Be sure you know where your local veterinarian is.

 Daily check

1 That the dog has proper food and clean water.
2 That the dog has enough exercise.
3 That you groom the dog.
4 That you wash the food and water bowls.
5 That your dog's bed is clean.

 Weekly check

1 That you wash and dry the dog's bedding.
2 That you have enough food for the coming week.
3 That the dog's toys are not getting chewed up or are dangerous.

 Yearly check

1 That you have a license for your dog. Check local regulations, as they vary from place to place.
2 That your dog has boosters for its inoculations.

Questions and answers

Q How big is the biggest dog?

A The heaviest dog is the St. Bernard, which may weigh over 280 lb (127 kg). The tallest is the Irish wolfhound which may stand as much as 39 inches (1 m) at the shoulder.

Q Which is the smallest dog?

A The Chihuahua, which may weigh as little as 1 lb ($\frac{1}{2}$ kg) when full grown.

Q How long does a dog live?

A Very big and very tiny breeds generally have short lives. Medium sized dogs often live to twelve years or more. The oldest known dog, a labrador, lived for over 27 years.

Q How fast can a dog run?

A A greyhound can sprint at over 41 mph (66 km/h) for a short distance. Salukis can run nearly as fast but keep up for longer. Several long legged breeds can run at over 30 mph (48 km/h).

Q What is the scientific name of the dog?

A *Canis familiaris.*

Q Does my dog understand when I talk to him?

A Dogs can learn to understand many words, but not whole sentences. They are very quick to pick up general meaning in your tone of voice, and also in your body language.

Index

PRINTED IN BELGIUM BY
proost
INTERNATIONAL BOOK PRODUCTION